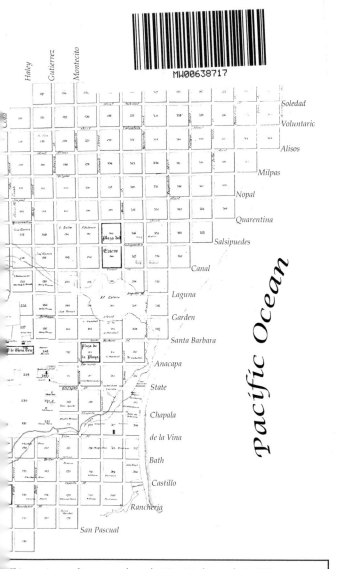

Haley
Guerrez
Montecito

Cota

Soledad
Voluntario
Alisos

Milpas

Nopal

Quarentina

Salsipuedes

Plaza de
Estero

Canal

El Estero

Laguna

Garden

Santa Barbara

Plaza de
la Playa

Anacapa

P de Obra Cruz

ESTADO

State

Chapala

de la Vina

Bath

Castillo

Rancheria

San Pascual

Pacific Ocean

This map is one of two maps drawn by Vitus Wackenreuder in 1853, two years after Salisbury Haley surveyed the city and created the grid of streets and blocks.

The center of the city was the subject of a second map that clearly showed where the newly plotted streets passed through private property and adobes, most of which had been granted and built in the Mexican era long before the survey. Even so, for the most part the streets and blocks existed only as wooden stakes marking their location. It would be decades before many of the streets were graded and opened for use.

Published Nov. 2008
Printed in Canada
ISBN: 978-0-9821636-0-3

PRODUCTION
Design & Layout: Anna Lafferty of
    Lafferty Design Plus, Santa Barbara
Illustrations: Vanessa Conejo
Cover Design: Annie J. Dahlgren
Publisher: El Barbareño Publishing

PHOTOS
Photos pp 26, 28, signature p43 courtesy Santa Barbara
    Historical Museum. Signatures pp38, 39 from *California
    Calligraphy*, Fr. Maynard Geiger O.F.M. Signatures pp
    27, 31 *Gateway to Alta California - The Expedition to San
    Diego*, 1769, Harry W. Crosby. Carpintería Cemetery.
    (Neal was portraying William Wyles at the Santa Barbara
    County Genealogical Society's "Picnic in the Cemetery.")
All other photos and maps from author's collection.

Front cover: Looking down Mission Street from Laguna
    towards Garden c1896.
Inside front cover: Map of Santa Barbara by Vitus
    Wackenruder, April, 1853.
Inside back cover: View of Santa Barbara from 12,000 feet,
    January 21, 2002 (Pacific Western Aerial Surveys).
Back cover: A View of Santa Barbara (c1849) from
    California Illustrated by J. M. Letts, 1853.

www.elbarbareno.com
www.anniejdahlgren.com

STREET
NAMES
OF
SANTA BARBARA

by
Neal Graffy, XNGH

Dedicated to
Antonio Maria de la Guerra
Joaquin Carrillo
Eugene Lies
and
Salisbury Haley

Thanks to

Anna Lafferty – Anna has been such a delight to work with. Her design and layout are brilliant. No matter how the manuscript and artwork had changed each time we met, she got it all to fit. I'm looking forward to working with her on the next Santa Barbara Pocket History.

Vanessa Conejo – What a find! She was able to take my "visions" for the street art and produce amazing artwork far beyond what I was expecting.

Shirley Diamond – for making the first edit.

Dorothy Oksner - for tracking down loose ends. She can find a needle in a haystack!

Hattie Beresford…All I asked her to do was to read this and check for errors. I knew she was an excellent researcher and historian, but what I didn't know was she was a retired teacher and a grammar teacher at that. Hattie's red pen came out of retirement for three edits and I cannot thank her enough for her corrections, suggestions and encouragement.

Annie J. Dahlgren – She is not only my bookkeeper, producer, and editor, she is also my wife. She has read this (and heard me read this) so many times and never got tired of it. I'm keeping her.

STREET NAMES OF SANTA BARBARA
by Neal Graffy

A BRIEF HISTORY OF SANTA BARBARA

Santa Barbara lies in a unique setting; its coastline faces south allowing it to bask day long in the sun's east to west journey. To the north, a chain of mountains runs east/west – a rare event in North America – blocking cold winds from the north and inviting cool Pacific breezes which results in a warm year-round Mediterranean climate.

15,000 years ago – First evidence of human habitation, making Santa Barbara one of the oldest continuously occupied places on earth.

5,000 years ago – The Chumash culture emerges. Putting things into perspective, this was 500 years before the Great Pyramid was built and 2,000 years before Jerusalem was founded.

1542 – Santa Barbara is first viewed by Europeans as three ships under the command of Juan Rodriquez Cabrillo sail from Mexico to explore the uncharted coast of California.

1602 - Sebastian Vizcaíno explores the California coast searching for safe harbors for Spanish trade ships. On December 4, he bestows Saint Barbara's name to an island and the channel. During his voyage he also names San Diego, San Pedro, Point Concepción, Monterey and Santa Catalina, San Nicholas and San Clemente islands.

1769 – Gaspar de Portolá, governor of Baja California, leads an overland expedition from Loreto, Baja in search of Monterey Bay and passes through Santa Barbara in August.

1782 – The last of California's four presidios, the Royal Presidio of the Channel of Saint Barbara is founded on April 26 to protect the vast region between the presidios of Monterey and San Diego.

1786 – Mission Santa Barbara is founded on December 4.

1821 – Mexico wins its independence from Spain and takes possession of California.

1835 – Mission Santa Barbara is secularized, meaning the Indians are released from the mission system and the mission livestock and lands placed in the hands of an administrator. The bulk of the vast lands once held by the Franciscans in trust for the Chumash are soon granted to private citizens and the great rancho period begins.

1846 – The American flag is raised over Santa Barbara.

1872 – Stearns Wharf is completed. Ships can now safely tie up to discharge passengers, who had previously been rowed ashore, and cargo, which had been dumped overboard and floated in.

1876 – The 80-room Arlington Hotel opens, providing first-class lodging as Santa Barbara gains a reputation initially as a health resort and eventually as a tourist destination.

1887 – The first train arrives from the south. Connection to San Francisco by rail will wait until 1901.

1892-96 – Annual Flower Festivals bring thousands of tourists.

1903 – Milo M. Potter opens the luxurious Potter Hotel on 36 acres along West Beach. The 5-½ story hotel gains a worldwide reputation and puts Santa Barbara on the map as *the* place for the upper class to vacation. A number of guests buy property in nearby Montecito and establish magnificent estates.

1912 – The American Film Company opens a studio and cranks out over 1200 silent films over the next decade.

1916 – Brothers Allan and Malcom Loughead establish the Loughead Aircraft Manufacturing Company (later renamed Lockheed) and build seaplanes for the Navy.

1924 – The Old Spanish Days Fiesta is established to preserve the old songs, customs and costumes of days gone by and to present them to new generations in a five-day celebration of music, food, dance and parades.

1925 – On Monday, June 29 at 6:43 am, a 6.5 magnitude earthquake rocks the community. Though residential damage is slight and only eleven are killed, nearly the entire business section is destroyed. Strict building codes and the creation of an Architectural Review Board results in one of the world's most beautiful cities rising from the ruins.

1942-1945 - Sleepy Santa Barbara gets active during the War Years as tens of thousands of service men pass through the Marine Corps Airbase, rehabilitation hospital or one of the hotels taken over by the government for two-week furloughs.

After the war many who had visited – even some of the former prisoners at the nearby German and Italian POW camps – return to study at the new University of California at Santa Barbara, establish businesses, or work for the defense industries springing up to battle the Cold War.

1952 – The author is born. Unfortunately the birth is premature – by nine years – and he becomes a native of Kansas rather than Santa Barbara.

THE SURVEY AND
NAMING OF THE STREETS

In the beginning there were paths primarily trod by the Chumash Indians that led between villages and to springs, creeks and sources of food. When the Spanish arrived they added their own trails to water, pasture and grain lands. But whether Chumash or Spanish, all most likely had a name indicating where the trail led. Moving beyond the local transportation grid, the Spanish added *El Camino Reál* – The King's Highway – linking the missions, presidios and pueblos. Though hardly fit for a king and not quite a highway, it was a start.

For nearly a decade the non-native inhabitants of Santa Barbara dwelled within the confines of the presidio. No street names needed here - just yell across the plaza to your neighbor. In the 1790s as the first homes were built outside the presidio walls, necessity rather than an Architectural Board of Review or Planning Department dictated placement. Fertile soil, good drainage and availability of water were all the planning they needed. The result caused one early visitor to claim, "The town was laid out by means of a large blunderbuss loaded with adobe houses and discharged from the top of the hill."

Organization was to be laid over the chaos in early 1850 when the fledgling California legislature ruled that for a town to be incorporated it needed - among other conditions - to be surveyed and the boundaries established and recorded.

The Common Council of the City of Santa Barbara put out the call for a surveyor in December 1850, and after six weeks only one person had applied for the job – Salisbury Haley. Haley's experience as a surveyor is debatable as most of his 38 years had

Surveyors pose with their equipment c.1880

been spent as a sea captain along the East Coast and Florida Keys. But how hard could the job be? It seemed simple, survey the town "from the Mission Gardens to the sea and from hill to hill on each side" and, within that frame, create a grid of blocks 450' x 450' with streets 60 feet wide except for two *calle principals* to be 80 feet, one running east/west and the other north/south.

For years Barbareños and tourists alike have wondered why Haley didn't run the streets in the direction of the compass points. It wasn't Haley's call, the Council directed where his stakes would be when they spelled out the locations of the two main streets. The first would be "a few yards east of the usual landing place at the *playa* (beach), through a point about one yard from the southeast corner of the store of I. J. Sparks, and thence through a point about two feet northwest of the door of the west side of Don Joaquin Carrillo's residence. The second, at right angles with the first, running along in front of the corridor of the house occupied by the said Don Joaquin Carrillo." Thus State and Carrillo streets were established and the grid of streets would grow from there.

While Haley was busy with his survey, on February 22, 1851, the Council minutes recorded the next step: "Eugene Lies, Antonio Maria de la Guerra and Joaquin Carrillo were appointed a Committee to Name the Streets about to be laid down on the map of Salisbury Haley."

Eugene Lies, an attorney, was born in New York in 1820, educated in Paris and came to California in 1847. He was a gifted poet, writer, translator (in several languages including Spanish) and appointed to the first Grand Jury and elected to the Assembly. Twenty-six year old de la Guerra, the youngest son of Don Jose de la Guerra, had already served as secretary to the *ayuntamiento* (town council) in 1849 and would continue on as a State Senator, councilman, mayor, county supervisor and Captain of Company C of the California Volunteers during the Civil War. Joaquin Carrillo had also been a member of the *ayuntamiento* and would later be elected mayor and a councilman. Though he didn't speak or write in English, he was highly regarded as a county and district judge during the American period.

Unlike other towns whose streets bore the unimaginative A - Z, numbers, trees or names of presidents, these three men gave names to our streets that portrayed the geography and botany of our town, honored the Chumash, early settlers, governors, and at times, showed a distinct sense of humor and sarcasm.

This is the story behind the names.

THE ORIGINAL 52

GEOLOGICAL

These eight streets describe the natural features of Santa Barbara as seen and experienced by the early settlers. Some of these features no longer exist due to the hand of man. Others are hidden by homes, buildings and landscaping, but the names remain to remind us of what was once there.

Cañada - Spanish-English dictionaries translate this word as "glen, dale, dell, glade or cattle path." The early settlers used it to mean "ravine" or "small canyon." A multi-talented street, Cañada satisfies most of the above. Heading north, the street leads into a ravine (cut by Sycamore Creek) just past Quinientos Street. It starts up again at Montecito Street and terminates in the lower Riviera, an area of many small canyons, glens, dales and dells.

Canal - *¿El Calle Perdido? Si!* Missing from our city maps since the early twenties is Canal Street which is currently doing business as Olive Street.

Canal can mean channel, canal, or waterway which would not be a bad name for a thoroughfare in a yacht harbor, but what did it mean for a street here on *terra firma*?

Oddly enough, it may have been because this street was sort of a channel *above* a waterway. To the east and west of this street, the ground slopes downward. These low areas were often wet and boggy from creeks and springs and especially after the winter rains.

Therefore, you could head down Canal Street and not get your feet wet as it provided a safe "channel" to the Channel.

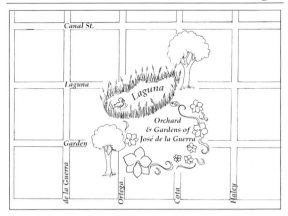

Laguna – The first name given to Santa Barbara was *Laguna de la Conceptión* due to a small lake (a *laguna* as the Spanish say) that once existed near the intersection of Laguna and Ortega streets. When the Portolá Expedition passed through here in 1769 they camped not too far away from the *laguna* and as it was about the most exciting and dominant feature they'd seen all day they named the area after the little lake.

Laguna Street is also said to have earned its name as it passed through "*El Estero*" the large estuary (or slough) that extended at its fullest from present day Milpas to Santa Barbara streets and from Anapamu to the beach. But the early maps definitely designate the features of *El Estero* and *Laguna* as distinct and separate entities. Therefore, as the street is named Laguna and not Estero, the little lake deservingly should get all the credit.

Montecito - Derived from two words, *monte* (hills or woods) and *cito* (small), the one word describes the vista of "little hills and woods" the Spanish saw before mansions and extensive landscaping took over.

Oddly enough, in contrast to the millionaire inhabitants of Montecito today, the first white settlers of that area were primarily ex-presidio soldiers who were given the land in lieu of their back pay.

The street however has remained indifferent as to who plods along its path. It earned its name simply by providing the passageway that led into *El Montecito*, as it still does today.

Pedregosa - Meaning "stony" or "rocky," *pedregosa* describes the natural terrain of the Upper East Side at that time. This abundance of rock, primarily sandstone, was a great source of building material and one of the factors in determining the location for Mission Santa Barbara. Even Mission Creek was originally called *Arroyo del Pedregosa* (*arroyo* meaning creek).

Santa Barbara is famous for its red-tiled roofs and white plaster, yet sandstone is seemingly unsung as part of the natural beauty and history. The Chumash created bowls, mortars and pestles from it, and from the Spanish era to this day, it has served as foundations, walls, stairs, hitching posts, walkways and curbing. Even the walls have tales to tell - the ethnicity of the stonecutters can be revealed in the styles, shapes and sizes of stone they used.

One of the earliest and best known stone masons was Joseph Dover (namesake, by the way, of Dover Road) who in the early 1890s built the beautiful walls running from behind the Mission around to the Museum of Natural History. Few of the thousands of motorists who pass by these walls realize the bridge they use to cross Mission Creek was built in 1891 by Dover and fellow mason, Joseph Wood, a testimony to the beauty, strength and endurance of *la pedregosa*.

Punta Gorda - A *punta gorda* can be a "high bluff or fat point" and this street originally ran across the base of a large bluff located roughly between the beach and today's Milpas and Por la Mar streets. (It may have also been a little play on words as Jose de la Guerra's "big bluff" was played out here - see Voluntario Street.)

Now covered with homes, trees and a hotel, the bluff has disappeared from our view and, unfortunately, the most important section of the street, along the bluff's base, from our maps. That portion was renamed Calle Puerto Vallarta in the 1980s to honor our sister city in Mexico.

Salinas – A *salinas* is a salt marsh and this road led straight to *las salinas* where the early settlers would go to gather salt. In the early 20th century there were plans to drain and deepen *las salinas* and turn it into a yacht harbor. The plans never came to fruition and in 1928 Miss Huguette Clark gave the city $50,000 to rehabilitate the property. The salt pond was drained, filled with fresh water, landscaped and renamed the Andrée Clark Bird Refuge in honor of Miss Clark's sister, who had died in 1920 at the age of 16.

Salsipuedes - This street comes with a warning – get out if you can! (*sal si puedes!*). It not only passed though portions of *el estero*, making for a difficult journey, but also led into a box canyon with a small stream running through it. The marshy terrain and sheer sides of the canyon would have been a challenge for anyone hapless enough to enter to *sal si puedes*.

In 1922 the new Santa Barbara High School was built on the flat land to the east above the rim of the little canyon. Apparently overlooked in the design for the campus was an athletic field. To the rescue came Frederick Forrest Peabody, president of the school board (and former head of the Arrow Shirt Company). Peabody bore the entire cost of $100,000 to transform the box canyon into a sports amphitheater which the grateful students of Santa Barbara High School named Peabody Stadium in his honor.

BOTANICAL

Today Santa Barbara is hailed as a "Tree City." From above it appears as a carpet of green accentuated by red tile roofs. Under the green canopy, flowers, bushes, shrubs and grasses provide a cornucopia of color. But it was not always so, for a large part of our landscape has been introduced from nearly every continent and island in the world. The sight that greeted the Spanish settlers was a rolling grassy plain punctuated here and there by groves of oaks, with alders and sycamores usually following the creeks. Upon viewing the site for the future presidio and mission, the venerable Father Junípero Serra said of Santa Barbara "...the place looks dismal and... has but little water." From this "dismal" landscape, our Committee of Three picked four plants to flourish as streets.

Alisos – Although technically *aliso* is the Spanish word for alder and *socomoro* the word for sycamore, *aliso* seems to have been the preferred word used for the sycamore by the explorers and settlers. Indeed, old maps of Santa Barbara show a "Valley of Los Alisos," a place that today we call "Sycamore Canyon."

The Western Sycamore (*plátanus racemósa*) is native to the Santa Barbara area and found along streams, rivers and washes. The Chumash used the large burls or knobs along the bottom of the trunk for making bowls. Spanish use of the sycamore for construction purposes met with limited success. The rafters and beams of the Mission were originally of sycamore, but as they were prone to rot and destruction by worms they were eventually replaced by pine. The Spanish did prize the sycamore for its wood in making their *carretas*, the wheels being fashioned from a solid piece from the trunk. Edwin Bryant in *What I Saw in California* (1849) described the carreta as "...the rudest specimen of the wheeled vehicle I have ever seen." Its wooden wheels creaking and screeching on the wooden axles signaled the approach of the carreta long before its arrival.

Today only one venerable giant sycamore stands at the corner of Alisos and Montecito streets where once a fine grove of trees stood.

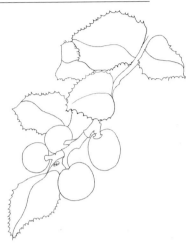

Islay - Also called the Evergreen Cherry and the Holly-leaf Cherry, the *islay (prunus ilicifolia)* can be a shrub about 4 to 7 feet high or a small tree as large as 25 feet high. The plant produces a small dark purple fruit, very sweet to the taste and used by the California Indians as a food. The seed kernels were also edible, but had to be boiled several times to leech out the cyanide they contained. The word *islay* is not Spanish, and probably not Chumash, but is the name the California Indians used for the plant.

It can be found along the hills and mountains from Southern California to Baja, the Santa Lucia Mountains along the Monterey Coast and as far north as the Napa Range. And though indigenous to the Santa Barbara area, you would be hard pressed to find one on Islay Street today.

Nopal – It can be a fruit, a vegetable, a tool, a medicine, and it can really hurt you. Who could imagine that the Prickly Pear cactus, a *nopal* in *español*, could be all this and more. Its thorny pads (*nopales*) and the equally thorny fruit (*tunas*) were eaten by the Chumash and early settlers. The thorns were, of course, removed beforehand. Wasting nothing, the Chumash used the very sharp thorns for piercing their ears and crushed the pads to make a salve or poultice for wounds, bruises or aches.

11

The Spanish planted it to create natural "barbed-wire" fences around gardens and orchards to keep out livestock, deer and other varmints. It was also an important part of home building. The liquid from crushed *nopales* was utilized as a bonding agent and water repellent in whitewashing adobes.

Reminiscences of early settlers state that when this street was surveyed, it passed through or near large stands of *nopal* thus accounting for the name. Today there is only one *nopal* along the street, growing in a garden at the corner of Nopal and Montecito streets.

Pitos – The Spanish word for whistle is *pitos,* and we find that this street, as originally surveyed, extended to Sycamore Creek and into marshland. And what does that have to do with whistles? Well, it would be here, along the creek and wetlands that one would find stands of carrizo grass. Growing as tall as 16 feet and an inch thick, its hollow stem was utilized for a number of purposes by the Chumash and most notably in our case, as flutes and whistles.

THE CHUMASH

Eight of the original fifty-two street names honor the Chumash, the name given to a group of Native Americans ranging from Malibu in the south to San Luis Obispo in the north. They were skilled hunters, fisherman, and, unique among Native Americans, builders of plank canoes. They utilized the tar from the natural oil seeps to seal their canoes, create watertight baskets and for many other uses. The last pureblooded Chumash, Tomás Ygnacio Aquino died in 1952.

Anacapa - One of two streets from the Chumash language, Anacapa is translated as "mirage" or "ever-changing." This accurately describes Anacapa Island which, depending on the day, time and mist conditions, can be viewed as no island, one island, or several islands.

The actual pronunciation of Anacapa is something like "on - ya - pah," but the name has certainly been muddled over the years. The English explorer Captain George Vancouver, during his stop here in 1793, described Anacapa in his log for Tuesday, November 19th as "...a group of three islands, called by the natives Enneeapah." In 1827 Frenchman Auguste Duhaut-Cilly, aboard the French trader *Heros* wrote, "...toward the southeast, is a cluster of four small islands called by the Indians 'Enecapah.' " The first maps showing the street names in 1853 used "Enecapap" as did the minutes of the Town Council. By 1854 the current spelling of "Anacapa" was in place.

Anapamu - The second of the two Chumash words to grace our streets, *anapamu*, means "rising place." In the old days, it would have been easy to see how the land here rose dramatically above the upper boundaries of the slough. You can still get the feeling for it today by driving (or preferably walking) west along Anapamu starting at Santa Barbara High School. As you pass by Peabody Stadium, note the twenty foot drop in elevation there and upon reaching Olive, look back and see the climb you've made. Another glimpse down Laguna and Garden towards the ocean pretty much says it all.

Like Anacapa, it took a little work to figure out how to spell this one. The two street maps of 1853, drawn by Vitus Wackenreuder, had "Anapanne" on one and "Anabanni" on the other while the Town Council preferred "Amnepamme." The following year, the Council appointed a committee to standardize the spelling of all the streets and "Anapamu" has been with us ever since.

The beautiful Italian Stone pines along this section of the street were first planted in 1908. Note how their roots wreak havoc on the sidewalks and streets thus ensuring that Anapamu will always be a "rising place."

Cacique – This word is not actually Spanish, but comes to us from the Caribbean courtesy of the natives who called their chieftains *"cacike"* or *"kassequa."* The Spanish quickly picked up on the lingo and used the word *"cacique"* for the chief or chieftain of any group of new world residents including, of course, the Chumash. Unlike Yanonali, this street did not lead to a village. So exactly which chief or chiefs this street is honoring is still unknown. What is known is the names of the nineteen Chumash chiefs and their villages as of March of 1796 when presidio comandante Felipe de Goycoechea recorded them and sent them to Governor Diego de Borica. So perhaps we can just say this street honors them all.

Carpintería – The street is named for the town 12 miles east of Santa Barbara, and the town is named for what the Portolá Expedition saw at the Chumash village of "Mishopshnow" on August 17, 1769. Located near the mouth of Carpintería Creek and the adjacent tar pits, there were about 300 inhabitants but more impressively, seven canoes. In his journal for the day Father Juan Crespí wrote , "…the village looked like a shipyard. The Indians were building a canoe, which was lacking the last plank at the top." Impressed with the Chumash boat building activity, the Spanish named the town *La Carpintería* – "the carpenter's shop."

Curiously, the streets bearing the names of towns east of Santa Barbara are in the same order as they are encountered - San Buenaventura, Carpintería and Montecito.

Indio Muerto - Literally "dead Indian," this street owes its name to the discovery of a deceased Indian found in the area during the time of the Haley Survey.

Ranchería - As most of our streets lead to or near their namesake, one could therefore expect this street to take us to a *ranchería*, the Spanish word for an Indian village or town. But no Chumash villages are known to have existed along Ranchería Street's nineteen blocks, which, as planned, started at Mason (that point now tennis court #4 in Pershing Park) and ended at Mission Street, the city limits in 1851. However, the old path that did pass for Ranchería Street did continue past Mission Street and led to the Chumash village of Cieneguitas. Located in the vicinity of today's Modoc Road and Hollister Avenue, it was one of the few Chumash sites still occupied at that time.

Most of Ranchería Street now lies under US Highway 101. Only two blocks, the 300 and 400 between Montecito Street and Coronel Place remain.

Valerio - Valerio Joseph was a Chumash Indian born at Mission
Santa Barbara on August 6, 1792. Unhappy with life at the Mission, he ran away and found refuge in a cave in the foothills above
Santa Barbara. According to legend, he was given powers from
spirit helpers that rendered him invisible, allowing him to enter the
pueblo undetected and liberate supplies and food for his survival.
In September of 1827, he killed an Indian named Wenceslau and
his powers were lost.

Eventually his hideout was discovered and he was soon surround-
ed by presidio soldiers and Chumash Indians. An archer fired first,
piercing him under the shoulder. Defiantly, he pulled the arrow
out and flung it back at his attackers. Three more arrows and two
bullets quickly found their mark and Valerio breathed his last. He
was buried at the Mission on March 16, 1828.

Twenty-three years after his death, Valerio was deemed worthy
enough to be remembered for all time with a street bearing his
name and, possibly pointing the way to his hideout.

Yanonali - Yanonali was chief of one of the largest Chumash villages and was said to have authority over 12 other villages. He was friendly towards the Spanish and provided workmen to help them build their presidio after they arrived here in 1782.

Though many of his people converted to Catholicism, he held out until September 12, 1797. His Baptismal record for that date lists his age as 60 and notes that he was chief of the village of Syukhtun and gives his baptismal name as Pedro.

Though a Catholic, he perhaps would have been more at home with one of the early tenets of the Latter Day Saints. Pedro had three and possibly four wives! One wife was Anastasia, whom he married the same day he and she were baptized. Another wife was Cecilia who died in 1798, probably after hearing of his other marriages! Keeping a distance between the wives seemed a good idea, so he had one wife on Santa Cruz Island and another one in the Santa Ynez Valley. He died smiling and exhausted on April 4, 1805.

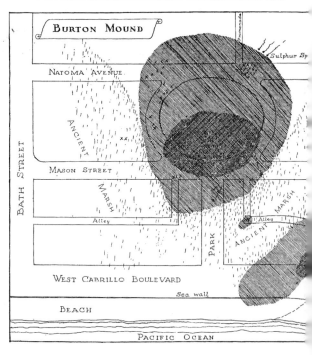

Yanonali Street leads to his old village of Syukhtun which means "where two trails run" in Chumash. The village was situated on a large mound about 30' high, located approximately between present day Bath, Chapala, West Cabrillo Boulevard and Yanonali Streets.

Burton's Mound - In the 1820s an adobe was built on the mound and, at various times, owned or occupied by a veritable Who's Who of early seamen and otter-hunters including Joseph Chapman, Thomas Robbins, Isaac Sparks, George Nidever and its namesake, Lewis T. Burton. Burton sold it in 1875 to the Seaside Hotel Company (who never built a hotel) and for the next 25 years it was pretty much the unofficial picnic grounds of Santa Barbara where many grand celebrations and parties were held.

Milo M. Potter bought the mound and, in 1903, opened the magnificent Potter Hotel on the 36-acres which soon put Santa

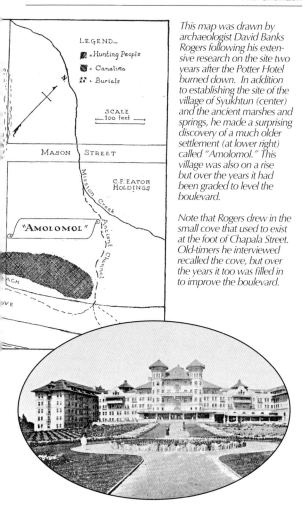

LEGEND—

🔲 = Hunting People

⬤ = Canalino

⚲ = Burials

SCALE
⟵ 100 feet ⟶

MASON STREET

Mission Creek

C.F. EATON HOLDINGS

Ancient Channel

"AMOLOMOL"

BEACH

OVE

This map was drawn by archaeologist David Banks Rogers following his extensive research on the site two years after the Potter Hotel burned down. In addition to establishing the site of the village of Syukhtun (center) and the ancient marshes and springs, he made a surprising discovery of a much older settlement (at lower right) called "Amolomol." This village was also on a rise but over the years it had been graded to level the boulevard.

Note that Rogers drew in the small cove that used to exist at the foot of Chapala Street. Old-timers he interviewed recalled the cove, but over the years it too was filled in to improve the boulevard.

Barbara on the map as a destination resort town. The hotel, which had been sold in 1919 and renamed The Ambassador, burned to the ground in April 1921, and the former hotel site was eventually filled in with streets, homes, and motels.

Flanked by palm trees planted in the teens, little Ambassador Park follows the grand entrance that once led to the hotel.

THE PATRON SAINT
OF OUR CITY

 W ho was Saint Barbara?

While there are many stories about Saint Barbara, most agree
on the information as presented below.

Saint Barbara lived in the third century in Asia Minor. Born
into a wealthy pagan family, she converted to Christianity after
learning of it from one of her tutors. When her father added a
tower to their home, she convinced the builders to change the
design from two windows to three windows to secretly repre-
sent the Holy Trinity. When her father found out, he was not
too pleased as being a Christian was against the law. Barbara
refused her father's demands to renounce her new-found faith,
so he brought her before the local magistrate hoping he could
convince her. Still she refused to give up her belief and was
severely tortured. She prayed for strength, endured the pain and
would not renounce her faith. During the night the marks of
torture miraculously disappeared. Upon viewing her the next
morning, the magistrate declared the gods had cured her, but
Barbara stood her ground and credited the one true God as her
healer. At this point she was condemned to death with another
night of torture to precede the execution. Her father was given
the honor of beheading her. Upon completion of the task,
though it was a clear day, he was struck by lightning and killed,
as was the judge who had sentenced her.

The name Santa Barbara was given first to the channel in 1602
by the Spanish explorer Sebastián Vizcaíno. Entering the channel in early December his ships encountered heavy fog which
cleared the following day and revealed two islands. The first
was named San Nicolás, for Saint Nicholas whose feast day
was December 6. The second island as well as the "passage
between the mainland and a group of islands" was named
Santa Barbára for the saint whose feast day was celebrated on
December 4.

Though the channel and the island bore her name, as noted in
the entry for Laguna Street, the site of our future city was known
as La Laguna de Concepción. This name quickly faded away
following the establishment of the presidio and mission. The
presidio was founded in April of 1782 as the "Presidio of the
Channel of Saint Barbara" and the mission, though founded
in December of 1786, had been planned and named for Saint
Barbara several years prior to the presidio founding. Thus, in a
one-two punch, the name La Laguna was knocked out and St.
Barbara reigned supreme.

Gaspar de Portolá

Portolá – The purpose of the "1769 Portolá Expedition" was to establish a military and spiritual presence in Upper California with *presidios* (forts) and missions at San Diego and Monterey.

Dubbed "The Sacred Expedition," it was a monumental undertaking of three ships and two overland groups that were to leave La Paz and Loreto, Baja California and meet in San Diego, a place that only existed as a name drawn on a map by Vizcaíno some 167 years earlier. Heading the expedition was the first governor of California, Gaspar de Portolá, and joining him was the new president of the California missions, Fr. Junípero Serra.

The first ship left in early January, and, due to bad winds, took three and a half months to reach San Diego. The second, the *San Antonio*, took nearly two months having missed San Diego and reached the Santa Barbara Channel before turning around. The third ship was never seen again. The overland groups took only six weeks (see Ortega for part of the story), but by the time Portolá arrived in late June, the situation was anything but a blessed one. Though the presidio had been founded by the first overland group, sixty of the ninety men aboard the two ships had died, mostly from scurvy. This was a large blow as many were skilled tradesman, desperately needed for the planned missions and presidios.

Despite the setbacks, Portolá left San Diego (Serra stayed behind to found the first of the California missions) and headed north in search of Monterey Bay which he missed. The following year he set out again from San Diego and this time located the bay and established the Monterey Presidio and Mission San Carlos.

The Portolá Expedition also left its mark on our county maps. In addition to Carpintería, we know where they saw a skinny bear (an *oso flaco*), met a Chumash chief with a crippled leg (*cojo* means lame) and shot a seagull (a *gaviota*). While the *San Antonio* was in the Santa Barbara Channel, (thinking the islands were the Coronado Islands) a priest went ashore and lost his staff which had a cross at the top. An Indian found and returned the staff and the thankful padre named the island Santa Cruz (Holy Cross).

As for California's first governor and overland explorer, his name can be found on Portolá Lane, a small street off Modoc Road by Las Positas and a stone's throw from Highway 101.

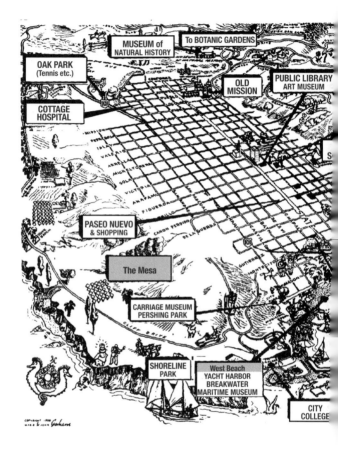

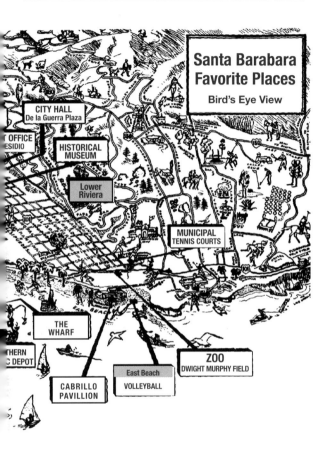

Santa Barabara Favorite Places

Bird's Eye View

CITY HALL
De la Guerra Plaza

OFFICE
ESIDIO

HISTORICAL MUSEUM

Lower Riviera

MUNICIPAL TENNIS COURTS

THE WHARF

THERN
C DEPOT

CABRILLO PAVILLION

East Beach
VOLLEYBALL

ZOO
DWIGHT MURPHY FIELD

This map was drawn by Marie and John Gorham in 1939 and soon after updated as a map for servicemen in WWII. We removed a few of the attractions from that era (including "Pick-up Stations for Servicemen") added a few new ones, and just for fun, left a few long-gone landmarks in place. After the passing of 60 years though, it was interesting to see how little Santa Barbara had changed.

FIRST FAMILIES

In 1851 when the streets were named, there were at least twenty-nine family names that dated back to the early presidio years and dozens more added in the 1800s. But only five names were destined to be remembered for all time. While it can't be said for sure what they were thinking when they made the selection, it is clear that each name is equally important in our history though for very different reasons.

Carlos Antonio Carrillo

Carrillo - Regarded by many historians as the leading family of early California. The patriarch of the family, José Raimundo Carrillo, was born in Loreto, Baja in 1749 and came to upper California in 1769 with the Portolá Expedition. He was first assigned to the San Diego Presidio and would ultimately rise in the ranks to serve as *comandante* of the Monterey, Santa Barbara and San Diego presidios.

In 1781, while stationed at the Monterey presido, he married Tomasa Ingnacia Lugo at Mission San Carlos, with the founder of the California missions, Father Junípero Serra, performing the ceremony. Two years later the Carrillos were sent to Santa Barbara where Carlos Antonio, the first of their seven children, was born.

Carried on by the children and grandchildren of José and Tomasa, the Carrillo name blankets the history of California from the Spanish through the Mexican and into the American era. Marriages into the best California families and with early American settlers formed a web of power and political intrigue. Whatever happened in California, a Carrillo was either leading it or pulling the strings behind it.

Carrillos were in the Mexican Congress, California (Mexican era) assembly, legislature, and, albeit for a very brief period, one was governor. During both the Mexican and American eras they were city councilmen of Santa Barbara and *alcaldes* and mayors of Santa Barbara, Los Angeles and Santa Monica.

The home of Judge Joaquin Carrillo once stood at the northeast corner of Carrillo and State streets.

Cota - One of the oldest Santa Barbara families, the Cotas, though certainly not carrying the political clout of the Carrillos or the de la Guerras, provided something even more important to the survival of the pioneers and the success of the settlements – women. They were probably the most important commodity in early California, especially if they were young and fertile. Between the four male Cotas (with a little help from their wives) they produced 31 daughters, resulting, it could be said, in California's first baby boom as the daughters came of age, married and started families.

The first Cota to step foot onto Alta California soil was Pablo Antonio, a soldier with the Portolá Expedition of 1769. He was present at the founding of the San Buenaventura Mission and the Santa Barbara Presidio. Pablo selected the site for Mission La Purisima Conception and headed the expedition to locate the site for the San Fernando Mission. Pablo and his wife had three sons and six daughters.

Pablo's brother Roque also came up from the presidio at Loreto, Baja. He settled in Los Angeles along with his wife and six daughters and got busy adding three California daughters to the brood starting in 1780.

Pablo Antonio de Cota

Roque's two sons, Mariano and Guillermo, rounded out the Cota sires. All, by the way, were in the military. Mariano was with his uncle Pablo for the founding of Mission San Buenaventura and possibly at the Santa Barbara Presidio founding, too. Mariano's marriage in 1788 was the fifth wedding performed at the presidio chapel, a union that would produce four sons and seven daughters. Guillermo took his time and didn't get married until 1794 when he was 26. Three decades and two wives later, two males and nine females had been added to the Cota clan.

The succeeding generations of Cotas left their mark in the annals of California too. Joaquin, the son of Mariano was involved in an unsuccessful revolt in 1829 to remove the Mexican appointed Governor, José Marie Echeandía, along with other officials and replace them with Californians. Another of Mariano's sons, Valentin, a corporal stationed at Mission Santa Inés, struck an Indian sparking the Chumash uprising of 1824. Valentin and his son, Pacifico, were among the participants in the *canon perdido* episode, an incident which would result in three more of our original street names. On a more positive note, members of the family also served as justices of the peace, administrators at the missions, members of the town councils in Santa Barbara and Los Angeles, as well as *alcalde* (mayor) of Los Angeles.

José de la Guerra

de la Guerra – Facing de la Guerra Street between State and Anacapa is Casa de la Guerra, one of Santa Barbara's grandest adobes, and home, likewise, to one its grandest families.

The de la Guerra story begins with the birth of José de la Guerra in 1779 in Spain. At thirteen he came to Mexico to live with an uncle, a well-to-do merchant. Forsaking a possible career as a priest or taking over his uncle's business, he applied for entry into the Royal Army of Spain in 1798. Due to his noble birth, he was accepted. In 1800 he was assigned to the presidio at Monterey where Raimundo Carrillo was *comandante,* but, more importantly, where he first set eyes upon Maria Antonia Juliana Carrillo, the fifteen-year-old daughter of the *comandante.* They were wed in 1804, uniting what would become two of the most powerful and influential families in California. Over the next eleven years the de la Guerras moved from presidio to presidio as José's military career advanced. The nomad army life came to an end in 1815 when he was appointed the fifth *comandante* of the Santa Barbara Presidio and they moved for the last time.

In 1819 de la Guerra commenced upon the construction of Casa de la Guerra, a project that would take nearly a decade and would house Don José and Maria Antonia's thirteen children (a project that would take them a little over two decades.) Casa de la Guerra soon became the centerpiece of Santa Barbara's social life and no visitor came away without writing of the graciousness and generosity of the de la Guerra family. A beautiful example of their sociability - the wedding of de la Guerra's daughter, Ana Maria, to hide and tallow merchant Alfred Robinson – was recorded by Richard Henry Dana in his book *Two Years Before the Mast,* an account of California life in the 1830s.

Of the thirteen sons and daughters of de la Guerra much can be said and they certainly contributed to distinguishing the family name that honors this street. Marriage connected them to prominent California families, as well as Americans and Spaniards.

Several sons were members of the *ayuntamiento* and *alcaldes*. Though some were bitterly opposed to American possession of California, they quickly became leading politicians of the new state. Pablo helped draft the California Constitution and was a state senator, lieutenant-governor, judge, county supervisor and mayor. Antonio Maria was also a state senator, county supervisor, councilman, mayor and Captain of the Native Cavalry during the Civil War. Still other sons were councilmen, mayors, judges and sheriffs.

Gutierrez –Compared to the other "street families," Octaviano Gutierrez was really a Juanny-come-lately and certainly didn't seem to have the pedigree or influence either. But he had something about him that led the Committee to by-pass the Ruiz, Lugo, Rodriguez, Gonzales and other early families and honor his name with a street.

He was born around 1800 in Mexico, joined the army, became a cannoneer and was assigned to the Santa Barbara Presidio. His arrival date is said to have been as early as 1816, but that he was here at least by 1824 is noted by a commendation for his valor during the Chumash uprising in February of that year. In 1827 he married Maria Celedonia Ruiz, the daughter of a presidio solider, at Mission San Buenaventura. Eleven months later the first of their 11 children was born and another 24 years would pass before the last of their brood arrived in 1851.

The Gutierrez home, built a few years after his marriage, stood along the east edge of De la Guerra Plaza nestled between two of California's most powerful families. At one end of the plaza was the grand Casa de la Guerra and flanking the opposite end of the plaza were the adobes of Carlos Antonio Carrillo and his brother, Pedro Carrillo.

Octaviano retired from the military in the early 1840s, and in 1845 he asked for and received from Governor Pio Pico, Rancho La Laguna, a 48,704 acre land grant in the Santa Ynez valley. A year later, Gutierrez was named Justice of the Peace for the Santa Inés district. With that, Gutierrez, after a life time of military service, seemed to embark on a new career of public service. He served on the first Grand Jury and in September 1851, was elected to the Santa Barbara Common Council (forerunner of the City Council). He was one of the first to complain about the Haley Survey, asking that it be annulled as he then proceeded to build a house in the center of one of the newly created streets!

Ortega – When José Francisco de Ortega first saw Santa Barbara in 1769, he had no idea that thirteen years later a presidio would be established here and its success or failure would fall fully on his shoulders.

Born about 1734 in Mexico, he enlisted in the army in 1755 and was assigned to the presidio at Loreto, Baja California. After 14 years he left the military and for a brief period tried his hand at mining. He returned to the service and distinguished himself in 1769 when he accompanied Governor Gaspar de Portolá in the overland trek from Loreto to Alta California to establish the first of the California missions and presidios and to find Monterey Bay.

The first 400 miles of the journey were along the Jesuit Trail linking the missions of Baja. The next leg of the journey, some 240 miles, would take them west across Baja to the Pacific and then north along the coast where they hoped they would recognize from the land side what Vizcaíno had described from the ship side as San Diego Bay. This was unexplored territory and Ortega was continually ahead of the main party, seeking and blazing the path that would carry them forward. After arriving safely at San Diego, they headed north in search of Monterey Bay, again armed only with Vizcaíno's description from 165 years earlier. Their 400 mile journey carried them through Santa Barbara where they found the natives to be gracious and generous, and to Monterey which they failed to recognize. But Ortega, the scout, is credited with being the first to discover the bay that made their objective pale in comparison – the great bay of San Francisco.

As noted earlier, Ortega was at the founding of the Santa Barbara Presidio on April 21, 1782 and was the first *comandante* from 1782 to 1783. Ortega and his men started with nothing but the empty plain of Santa Barbara. Shelter, defense, water, and good relations with the Chumash were all Ortega's responsibility and in this he succeeded. He retired in 1795 after serving as *comandante* of the presidios at Monterey and Loreto.

He returned to Santa Barbara and received one of the few ranchos "granted" during Spanish rule. His rancho, *Nuestra Señora del Refugio* (Our Lady of Refuge), covered over 26,000 acres stretching some 21 miles along the Gaviota coast from Refugio to the edge of Cojo and from the ridge of the mountains to the sea. He was married to Maria Antonia Victoria Carrillo (aunt of Raimundo Carrillo), and, though their descendants were numerous with several serving in the town councils during the Mexican and early American periods, it is likely that the Committee to Name the Streets honored the Great Pathfinder himself with Ortega Street.

A Few Translations

Alta California - Upper California (now the State of California)

Baja California - Lower California.

Presidio - Fort. The first presidio in the Californias was built at Loreto in Baja California in 1697. In Alta California there were four: San Diego (1769), Monterey (1770, San Francisco (1776) and Santa Barbara (1782).

Comandante - Commander of the presidio.

Alcalde - A combination of mayor, judge, and chief of police.

Ayuntamiento - The town council.

Barbareño - A resident of (where else) Santa Barbara.

DONDE EL CAMINO LLEVAR
(WHERE THE ROAD LEADS)

These streets evoke the events, places and sights that were familiar to, and part of the life of, the early settlers.

Bath - Originally labeled *Baños,* Spanish for bath, this street led to the West Beach area where townspeople would go to bathe as indoor plumbing was decades away. The street also passed the area known as "Burton's Mound" where hot sulpher springs were available for soaking.

Castillo - A *castillo* can be a castle or just a fortification. Qualifying for the latter definition, in the early 1800s a *castillo* was carved into the edge of the cliff overlooking and protecting the anchorage at West Beach. Though nearly a quater mile away, Castillo Street was named as it was the closest street to the little fort. Below the *castillo*, a large rock outcropping known as Castle Rock rose above the surf, and, though for many years a great tourist attraction, it was removed during the breakwater construction in the late 1920s. The site of the *castillo* was erased by the extension of Cabrillo Boulevard past Castillo in the early 1940's.

Chapala – You won't find this word in any Spanish dictionaries, but you will find a Lake Chapala and nearby a town of the same name in the state of Jalisco, Mexico. There are many theories as to the origin of the word ranging from a place where clay pots (*chapatla* in the native language) are made, to Chapalac, the name of the chief who ruled in that area in 1531 when the Spanish arrived there. Over the years the word evolved and was put to use to mean to "splash" or "paddle about" which were certainly activities quite common at Lake Chapala.

With that usage in mind, the word was correctly applied to the street bearing that name as the foot of Chapala Street was the scene of much "splashing" and "paddling about" for this was where sailors used to land and load their rowboats and skiffs with passengers and goods.

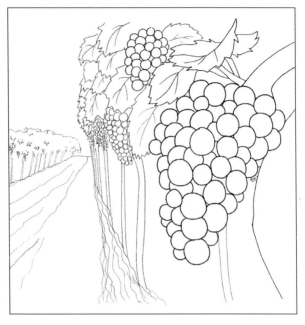

de la Viña – A *viña* is a vineyard and according to legend, one was planted by presidio *comandante* Felipe de Goycoechea in 1802 somewhere in the area near this street.

Legend or not, that someone had a vineyard in the area shows up in records during the Mexican period where the legal boundaries of several properties were described as being "between the race course and the *arroyo de la viña*." A little loose by today's standards, but back then everyone obviously knew where the *viña* was. Another claimant for the vineyard origin, though possibly after the fact, is Pascual Botiller, the son of a presidio soldier. Pascual had a vineyard, a small press and winery in the general vacinity. His two-story adobe, built around 1843, still stands at 1023 Bath Street.

So while we can't say for sure who planted first, we can agree that this was an ideal place for grapes. By the 1860s, nearly 200 acres of the West Side (over 40 city blocks!) were planted in vines. Today, houses and apartments cover the former vineyards and only the street name remains to tell us of what once was.

Garden – Sometimes seen on early maps as its Spanish equivalent, *Jardines*, this street passed through the de la Guerra family's garden which was roughly between Ortega and Cota Streets (see Laguna Street map on page 7). Water for the garden was handily supplied by several springs, and, also conveniently nearby, was *la laguna* (the little lake).

Milpas - Truly a New World word, *milpa* is a corn or maize field, a crop unknown in Spain. Tradition states that this was the area where the presidio soldiers had their maize fields, hence the plural, *milpas*.

Mission - The survey undertaken by Mr. Haley was to cover "from the Mission Gardens to the sea and from hill to hill on each side." Mission Street marks the boundary between what were the vast Mission lands and the pueblo of Santa Barbara.

Quarantina - This street name has been anglicized (and rather poorly at that) from the Spanish *cuarentena* which can mean "forty days, months or years." In this instance, the word means forty days, the standard period of isolation for plagues and other illnesses, and recalls two incidents in the 1790s where ships, one with scurvy and the other with smallpox, were placed into quarantine at the foot this street.

Soledad - The word *soledad* signifies a place of solitude or loneliness. The area around this street was so far out of town and uninhabited that the name was a perfect fit.

San Buenaventura - This street was the most southeastern street of the original grid, and even though it was just four blocks long, it was the street you'd be on as you left town to head down to San Buenaventura (now just Ventura).

Sadly the little pathway is no longer with us, having been run over by US Highway 101, crossed by the Southern Pacific railroad tracks, covered by a portion of Dwight Murphy field, Santa Barbara Zoological Gardens and a 1920s housing development.

Voluntario - This street led to the hill between East Beach and Milpas, Por la Mar, and Punta Gorda streets that was once known as *"Cerrito de los Voluntarios"* or "Hill of the Volunteers." The name has its origins in 1818 when Hippolyte de Bouchard sailed into Santa Barbara with the intent of sacking the town as he had done in Monterey and at the Ortega Rancho at Refugio. Bouchard, a Frenchman, is commonly referred to as a "pirate," but actually he was a "privateer" or mercenary hired by the Argentine government in their war for independence from Spain. Any Spanish ship or town was fair game to Bouchard and thus he anchored his two ships, *La Argentina* and the *Santa Rosa,* off Santa Barbara on the evening of December 8th.

Presidio Comandante José de la Guerra was hopelessly out-manned and outgunned by Bouchard's force of over 350 men and 62 ship's cannon. Bouchard had sent de la Guerra a note offering to spare the town if de la Guerra would return three of Bouchard's men captured during the Ortega Rancho raid, and, in turn, Bouchard would surrender prisoners he had taken at Monterey. Stalling for time, de la Guerra replied he would have to wait several days to get Governor Sola's permission.

This condition Bouchard found unacceptable, and he threatened to land immediately. De la Guerra replied that his men were more than willing and waiting. What Bouchard didn't know was de la Guerra had at best some 50 men.

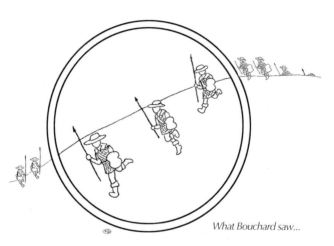

What Bouchard saw...

During the two days of negotiations, Bouchard, viewing from his telescope aboard ship, had clearly seen a steady stream of reinforcements from the south cresting the top of the hill at East Beach and heading towards the presidio. However, this was actually de la Guerra's small force of presidio soldiers and volunteers marching up the back side of the hill, along the top and then back down out of view to circle around again. De la Guerra's bluff worked! Bouchard agreed to exchange the prisoners and he sailed off without a shot being fired.

Voluntario now ends at Highway 101, but as originally plotted, the base was at the back side of the hill just below the intersection of Por la Mar and Orella del Mar streets. Covered today with trees, apartments, motels, and a hotel, the "Hill of the Volunteers" is well hidden. But a sense of it can still be discovered by viewing it from the East Beach Volleyball Courts or from Dwight Murphy field.

GOVERNORS OF CALIFORNIA

From a field of nine Spanish governors, fourteen Mexican governors, seven American Military governors and one California State governor, only four were picked to grace our street names. (Technically, we could include Carlos Antonio **Carrillo**, "San **Andres"** Pico, and Col. Richard. B. **Mason** to the list, but they are "streets" for other reasons.) Up until 1804 the governors ruled over two Californias, Baja (lower) and Alta (upper). Alta California is now the State of California.

With such a broad field to choose from it is quite interesting to see which ones they chose and speculate as to why.

Arrellaga - José Joaquin de Arrillaga [Arrellaga] held the office of governor longer than any in our history. He was lieutenant governor in 1792 when Gov. José Antonio Roméu died and thereupon became governor ad interim until 1794 when Diego de Borica was appointed. Upon Borica's death in 1800, Arrellaga again assumed the role of governor. Finally, the King officially appointed him governor in 1804. In 1809, he asked to be relieved of his duties and retire; instead he was promoted to the rank of Colonel. He died in office in 1814 and was buried at Mission Soledad. He was the first governor to rule over upper California.

Solá - Lt. Colonel Pablo Vicente de Solá was the last Spanish Governor of California (August 1815 to April 1822) and the first Mexican Governor (April 11, 1822 to November 1822). He is remembered for his strong devotion to education, establishing schools at the presidios and towns. He left California in 1822 to serve as its representative in the Mexican Congress. He died in Mexico possibly in 1826.

Victoria – Lt. Colonel Manuel Victoria was the military commander of Baja California when he was appointed the fourth Mexican governor of Alta California in early 1831. Disagreeing with some of the last orders of his predecessor, José María de Echeandía, he revoked them (including the secularization of the missions).

Unfortunately his rule reflected a strict military authority rather than a civil authority and the former governor, Echeandía, along with other leading Californians, rose up against him. An army of revolutionists engaged Gov. Victoria and his troops at the Battle of Cahuenga Pass on December 4, 1831 resulting in Victoria being wounded, surrendering the governorship and returning to Mexico.

Victoria was the first, but would certainly not be the last California governor to be thrown out of office.

Figueroa - A Mexican brigadier-general, José Figueroa was in office from 1832 to 1835. Figueroa issued the proclamations to emancipate the Indians from the missions and to remove the missions from the control of the Franciscans. He died in Monterey in September 1835. Before he died, he asked to be buried at Mission Santa Barbara where his bones currently reside in a vault in the sanctuary. Historian H. H. Bancroft considered him "the best Mexican governor ever sent to rule California."

Micheltorena - Brigadier-general Manuel Micheltorena was governor of California from 1842 to 1845. He arrived in California with a "convict" army raised from the prisons in Mexico, which did not sit well with the Californians. Ordered to keep foreigners out of California, he instead befriended them, granting several ranchos to Americans. A populist revolution culminating in a bloodless battle at Cahuenga Pass removed him from office and sent him back to Mexico.

GLIMPSES OF THE MEXICAN WAR
1846 ~ 1847

Much as the Colonists of New England, though descended from British settlers and subjects of British rule, considered themselves Americans and not British, the people of California considered themselves Californians and not Mexicans. By the mid-1840s California was in turmoil. Mexico, struggling with its own internal problems was too far away to provide the leadership that was needed. The Californians, too, were tired of politically-appointed Governors from Mexico rather than native sons. There were three potential futures – independence, rule by Britain, or rule by the Americans. When the United States went to War with Mexico in 1846, the result was inevitable.

Chino - The site of the first victory of the Californians over the "foreigners" during the 1846 war is recalled by Chino Street. The name comes from the Rancho Santa Ana del Chino, a 22,234 acre grant given to Isaac Williams in 1841 and located at the southwest corner of San Bernardino County.

Though Benito (Benjamin Davis) Wilson had arrived in California in 1841, married into the Yorba family, and was owner of a large rancho, he sided with the American interest and was soon in command of 20 men. He had been ordered to guard the Cajon Pass in the event General José Castro might pass that way, but upon discovering that Castro was already gone and on his way to Mexico, he and his men went hunting instead. Running low on ammunition and supplies, they stopped off at Williams' Rancho del Chino in search of replenishment.

On the morning of September 27, they found themselves sur-rounded by 80 to 100 Californians. Several shots were fired resulting in the wounding of three of Wilson's men and the death of one Californian. After the roof of the house was torched, Isaac Williams came out with three of his children, asking that their lives be spared. (Their uncle, José del Carmen Lugo, was one of the leaders of the Californians.) Despite the current circumstances, a number of the Californians were friends of Wilson and they sug-gested that the outnumbered Americans surrender and promised no harm would come to them. They complied, were taken prisoner and safely escorted back to Los Angeles.

San Pascual – A seemingly saintly street, San Pascual bears the name of Saint Paschal Baylon, a Spanish Franciscan who died in 1592. But what is actually memorialized here is not the holy man, but an incident near the small Indian village of San Pascual about 25 miles northeast of San Diego.

The Battle of San Pascual took place just after dawn on December 6, 1846 when troops under the command of American General Stephen Watts Kearny engaged Californians commanded by Andrés Pico. Kearny had just arrived from Santa Fe, a thousand mile march, and though his men and animals were exhausted, cold, and wet, they confidently charged believing Pico's men (hardly a professional army) would flee. Unfortunately, the American assault was confused and their powder was damp. The Californians, superior horsemen and formidably armed with their long lances easily tore into them. After fifteen to twenty minutes of intense fighting, the Californians were finally routed when two cannon arrived at the battlefield. The Americans claimed a victory as they held the field of battle. Historians generally reflect differently on the outcome, noting the Americans suffered the loss of twenty-one dead and sixteen wounded, while Pico only had eleven wounded, none seriously.

Gillespie - A street named for a secret agent? Indeed, and not only a secret agent, Lieutenant Archibald H. Gillespie, was a U.S. Navy Marine and a hero at the Battle of San Pascual.

In the fall of 1845 President James Polk gave Gillespie "secret instructions" which he was to deliver to the U.S. Consul at Monterey, Thomas Larkin. Masquerading as an ill merchant traveling to regain his health, Gillespie crossed through Mexico, then to Hawaii before arriving in Monterey in April 1846. Exactly what Gillespie's message to Larkin was has never been revealed, but most historians agree it concerned the upcoming and foreseeable war with Mexico and Polk's desire to have California in the Union. Gillespie then set out in search of Lt. John C. Frémont of the Army's Topographical Corp who had recently been in California, ostensibly on a mapping expedition. Gillespie finally found Frémont in Oregon and relayed – it is assumed – Polk's instructions as 30 days later Frémont was in California and participating in the Bear Flag Revolt which declared California a free republic.

A month later, in July 1846, the official news arrived that the United States was at war with Mexico, and Gillespie, promoted to captain, joined Frémont's newly created California Battalion. In early September he was left in charge of the pueblo of Los Angeles, though only for a short time, as superior forces caused him to surrender the city and retreat to San Pedro. In December, having been sent from San Diego to meet Gen. Kearny, he was at the Battle of San Pascual and despite receiving three severe lance wounds, he managed to light the fuse to a cannon which turned back the advancing Californians and saved the American troops from further disaster. Gillespie must have been quick to recover for on January 9th he was commanding troops at the Battle of San Gabriel where he was wounded again, this time when a rifle ball struck his hip. On January 13th Andrés Pico met with Frémont and signed the treaty ending the War in California and sparing Gillespie from further damage.

San Andrés - San Andrés, literally "Saint Andrew" is really named for Andrés Pico. He was born in San Diego in 1810 where his father was a soldier at the presidio. Among his 9 siblings was Pio Pico who would be governor of California in 1832 and from 1842 to 1845. Andrés was involved in the various schemes and plots of California politics in the 1830s and 1840s, but his shining moment was at the Battle of San Pascual where he was in command of the victorious California troops. By default, he was technically the last governor of Mexican California serving for a grand total of three days before meeting with Frémont to draw up and sign the Treaty of Cahuenga to end the war.

His elevation to "sainthood" shows how admired he was by the Californians. Highly regarded by the Americans as well, Pico was elected to the State Assembly in 1851 and the Senate in 1860. He was brigadier-general of the state militia and commissioned major of the First Battalion of Native Cavalry during the Civil War, though he declined due to illness.

State - Usually the principle street leading into a town is simply named Main, Grand or Central. In our case they decided to honor the new state of California, opting for the shorter "State" rather than the actual name. A few early maps labeled it *Estado*, the Spanish equivalent. After the 1925 earthquake, as the city adopted the Spanish feel in earnest, they tried again with the fancier *Calle Estado* but it didn't catch on and the street remains simply State.

In considering a "Yankee" name to hang on a street sign there were actually quite a few to choose from. By 1830, when Santa Barbara's population was 645 souls, ten of them were Americans and the following decade would bring a dozen or so more. Most of them settled into the community, got married, bought or were granted land and started businesses and families. Of course, first – if they weren't already – they had to become Catholics, speak Spanish (the thoughts of forthcoming nuptial bliss a strong incentive) and become Mexican citizens. Excluding Governor Mason and Lt. Archibald Gillespie who are included in other categories, only two made the cut. One was an obvious choice and the other somewhat a surprise.

Tomas M. Robbins

Robbins - Thomas M. Robbins was born in Massachusetts around 1801. Like most of the early American settlers, he was a seaman aboard one of the many ships plying the California coast engaged in the hide and tallow trade, smuggling, selling provisions (legally and illegally) and some, if not all, of the preceding.

He arrived in California in the summer of 1823 as first officer on the *Rover*, an 83-ton schooner out of Boston. The previous year had taken him from Boston around the tip of South America to the Hawaiian Islands and then California. For the next two years, he sailed the coast of California picking up otter skins, and then to the Hawaiian Islands, the Philippines and China, trading, buying and selling along the way. By 1830 he had settled in Santa Barbara and opened a trading store on the small hill near the waterfront (later known as Burton's Mound) between the beach and the future Chapala, Bath, and Montecito streets.

In 1832 he gave up his Protestant ways and became a Catholic. He had great incentive for his conversion. He'd set his eyes on Encarnación Carrillo, the beautiful daughter of Cárlos Antonio Carrillo, and to marry he had to be Catholic and a Mexican citizen, as well. With all the prerequisites accomplished, Thomas and Encarnación were married in 1834 and soon set about producing a family which eventually totaled 11. Robbins was highly respected by the Mexican government who gave him an honorary commission as Captain in the Mexican Navy. In 1846 he was grantee of Santa Catalina Island and Rancho Las Positas y La Calera (today's Veronica Springs, Hidden Valley and Hope Ranch areas). The street bearing his name was the road taken to get to his ranch.

Haley - Haley Street takes its name from Salisbury Haley who performed the survey for Santa Barbara's first streets.

Born in New Hampshire in 1812, Haley went to sea at an unknown age and became a "Master Mariner" along the Atlantic seaboard and Florida Keys. As Master Mariner he was not just captain of the ship, the title meant he was qualified to pilot a vessel of any size and to any port.

He was married in 1841 and settled in Florida where a daughter was born two years later. His wife died not long after and the daughter was taken in by relatives. It is probably not unreasonable to speculate the arrangement was due to Haley being gone at sea for extended periods.

When the cry of "Gold in California" reached Florida, Haley headed for the gold fields. He was in the Stockton area for a while and then showed up in Santa Barbara in January 1851 to undertake the town survey which he completed in May.

Following the survey, Haley returned to the sea where he became well known as captain of the coastal steamers *Sea Bird* and *Goliah* in the 1850s. His brother Robert also piloted coastal steamers.

Haley was a man of many hats – in addition to his Captain's headwear, he appears to have been a doctor, a pharmacist, a lawyer, and, of course, a surveyor (at least once). In 1854 he married into the prominent Sepulveda family of Los Angeles and eventually settled down in the City of Angels where he spent the remainder of his years practicing law.

EL CAÑON PERDIDO
The Lost Cannon

Cañon Perdido, Mason and Quinientos streets have their origins in an episode regarding a "Lost Cannon" which was not so much lost as it was stolen...

On the night of April 5, 1848 five Barbareños - Jose Antonio de la Guerra, Jose "Chato" Lugo, Jose E. Garcia, Jose Dolores Garcia, and Pacifico Cota - decided to steal and hide a cannon that was lying on the beach awaiting shipment to Monterey. Their hopes were to have it available in the event an insurrection would be forthcoming to drive out the Americans. Using a team of oxen, they dragged it from the foot of future Chapala Street to present day Anacapa Street before it got stuck and the oxen too tired to take it any further. Thereupon, they buried it.

Captain Francis J. Lippitt, the commanding officer at Santa Barbara, was already nervous. His fears that the populace would rise against the garrison were heightened when the *alcalde*, Pedro C. Carrillo mentioned he had heard an "idle rumor" that Pablo and Francisco de la Guerra, along with several others, had been discussing a possible revolt. When he heard the cannon was missing, he knew death and insurrection were on the horizon. Greatly exaggerating the value of the cannon and its possible use, he bypassed his superior, Col. Jonathon Drake Stevenson in Los Angeles, and sent a messenger (at great expense) bearing the news directly to the Military Governor in Monterey – Col. Richard B. **Mason.**

Mason was of a cooler head and gave the community until May 31, ample time to return *"el cañon perdido."* When the deadline passed without the cannon's return, he issued an order that the town be "laid under a contribution of $500" (or ***quinientos pesos*** as the Spanish would say) as compensation for the loss of the cannon.

As originally laid out, Quinientos Street ran from Castillo to Salinas (partially following the trail of the cannon) so apparently the Committee to Name the Streets thought the episode so grand they placed Quinientos and Mason as the first two streets one came across when entering Santa Barbara. Interestingly, they placed Cañon Perdido between Carrillo and de la Guerra, perhaps as a hint of the direct and subtle involvement of these two families in the whole affair.

Not only is this story forever etched on our streets, but the first seal of the city of Santa Barbara was engraved "Vale Quinientos Pesos" which can be translated as "Value 500 pesos" or "Goodbye 500 pesos!"

As for the cannon, it resurfaced in 1858 when it was uncovered by a winter storm and was then hauled with great ceremony up to State and de la Guerra streets. Sometime before 1876 it was sold and taken to a foundry in San Francisco where it was melted for scrap.

INDEX AND
GRINGO PRONUNCIATION

Time and tongue have somewhat loosened a few names from their original Spanish pronunciation, and if you spoke them like a true Spaniard, no one would have any idea what you were talking about. We hereby present the current, accepted Barbareño way to pronounce the street names. In no time at all, people will think you've been here since 1968!

Salinas.. 9
    *suh-**lean**-us*

Salsipuedes.. 9
    *sal-see-**pway**-dess or sal-seh-**pway**-dess*

San Andres 42
    *san **ann**-dress*

San Buenaventura................................... 36
    *san bwain-uh-ven-**tur**-uh*

San Pascual 41
    *san pass-**qwall***

Santa Barbara 20

Solá.. 38
    ***so**-la*

Soledad 36
    ***so**-la-dad*

State 42

Valerio.. 16
    *vuh-**lair**-ee-oh*

Victoria 39

Voluntario 36
    *volun-**tare**-ee-oh*

Yanonali 17
    *yah-**nun**-all-ee or yah-no-**nall**-ee*

AUTHOR, AUTHOR

Neal Graffy is almost a Santa Barbara native, the result of a premature birth nine years too soon in Wichita, Kansas.

His love for Santa Barbara History began at age 13 when he started gardening and doing odd jobs for Mrs. Leontine Phelan, a descendant of the founder of the Santa Barbara Presidio, who lived in an adobe house built from the Presidio ruins.

In 1989 he gave his first slide show on Santa Barbara History and has since given well over 250 presentations on 19 different topics. He is no stranger to the printed page, having written for the *Santa Barbara News-Press, Santa Barbara Independent, Santa Barbara Magazine*, the Santa Barbara Historical Museum, the Trust for Historic Preservation and the Santa Barbara Genealogical Society.

In return, his expertise has been sought out by the media with countless appearances on local, state and national radio and TV. He has been featured in several documentaries including the Emmy Award winning *Impressions in Time*. He has appeared statewide on Huell Howser's *California Gold*, KCET TV's *Life and Times* and, nationally, on *This Old House*.

Neal has served as a Board Member of the Historical Museum, member (and chairman) of the Santa Barbara County Landmarks Commission, board member of the Mission Canyon Association, and president of the Santa Barbara Corral of Westerners. He is also a founding member of de la Guerra y Pacheco Chapter 1.5 of the Ancient and Honorable Order of E Clampus Vitus and an exNoble Grand Humbug of that esteemed organization.

In 2002, *Santa Barbara Magazine* pronounced him "One of 20 Santa Barbaran's to Watch." Two years later, he founded the Santa Barbara History Consortium, a not-for-profit corporation, established for the specific purpose of providing local history to a wide audience through film and video production, publishing and oral presentations.

He is married to Annie J. Dahlgren (whom he met at a bachelor auction) and they live quietly together with the radon in the Mission Canyon area of Santa Barbara.

Laguna

State

Chino